SKETCHING AT HOME

for those who are
just beginning

John Hamilton.

BLANDFORD

Blandford
A Cassell Imprint

Villiers House, 41/47 Strand
London WC2N 5JE

Copyright © John Hamilton 1991

First published 1991
Reprinted 1993

British Library Cataloguing in Publication Data
Hamilton, John *1919-*
  Sketching at home
  1. Drawings. Technique
  I. Title
  741

ISBN 0–7137–2304 1

Distributed in the United States by
Sterling Publishing Co., Inc.,
387 Park Avenue South
New York, NY 10016–8810

Distributed in Australia by
Capricorn Link (Australia) Pty Ltd
PO Box 665, Lane Cove, NSW 2066

Printed and Bound in Great Britain by The Bath Press

This book follows my *Sketching with a Pencil* (Blandford, 1989) and, again, is for those who really are just beginning and who feel that they need some guidance. So many people say 'I wish I could draw, but I've tried and find that I just can't'. What they are saying is that they started off by attempting something that was too difficult, made a mess of it and gave up hope.

I am convinced that this happens. We buy some equipment when on holiday (possibly not the easiest for a beginner to use), see a glorious view and decide to draw or to paint it. Disaster follows and the only thing that remains is loss of confidence and a feeling of frustration. If you have had such an experience, this book is to help you to start again.

I want to dispel two myths. First, no matter what you have heard or read, you do not need a lot of equipment. You are sketching with a pencil, so you will need a pad, pencils and a rubber. Second, sketching is not for holidays only. Sketching is for any time — the odd half hour in the day or an alternative to television in the evening. The more enthusiastic you become the easier it will be to find the time.

Whatever prompted you to pick up this book, do please heed one word of advice: don't start by attempting anything too difficult. The result may kill your enthusiasm stone dead. Keep it simple. That attractive view from your bedroom window of houses with odd roof angles can wait for a while. Settle for a quick sketch of the left hand chimney on the nearest roof. It will be just as much fun. But there are all kinds of subjects closer at hand.

I hope this little book will persuade you that you can have a lot of fun without even moving to the window, let alone to the great outdoors. Enjoy sketching the objects all around you in the house, and as your confidence increases so your drawing will improve.

John Hamilton
The Parade
St Mary's
Isles of Scilly, Cornwall

What sort of equipment will you need to begin with?

First of all, a SKETCH BOOK. It should have a stiff cardboard back which will give you a firm surface to lean on, for you will almost certainly be balancing it on your knees, and some form of spiral binding, so you can fold back the pages easily. A glued binding will tend to fall apart with use, particularly if the book gets wet. As to size, I rather prefer A4, which is the same size as this book, but choose one which is right for you. Don't skimp on quality.

A 12-inch clear plastic RULER is often useful and, for those times when you venture outside, a BULLDOG CLIP will stop the pages blowing about in the wind.

PENCILS come in a great variety of shapes and sizes: buy nothing but the best quality. They are usually graded from 6H, which is very hard and used mostly by draughtsmen, through to 6B which is very soft and black. I suggest you buy an HB, which is in the middle, and a 2B, 4B and 6B. HB means hard and black, H means hard and B black — an easy code to follow.

It is important to choose a good RUBBER. It should be soft and bungy and large enough not to become lost.

Your pencils need to be kept sharp, so you will require a KNIFE. A pencil sharpener is not as effective for this job as a Stanley type knife with a retractable blade. For keeping a really sharp point, you will need a strip of fine grade SANDPAPER.

That is all you need. For sketching in the home you can always use a chair or a stool so there is no need to buy a portable stool for the time being.

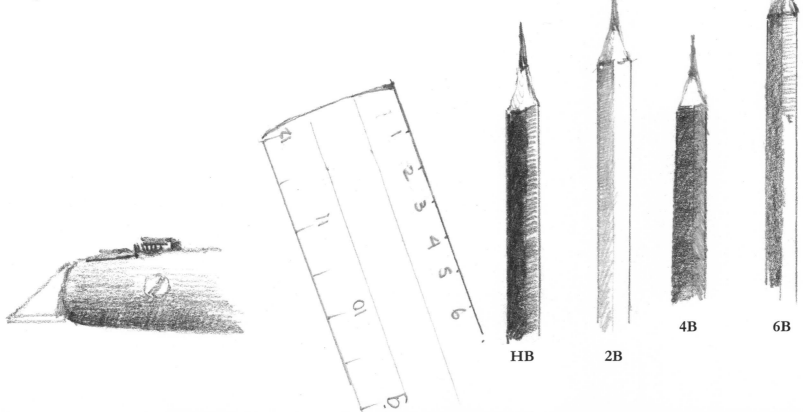

HB   2B   4B   6B

Before you start drawing, I am going to suggest that you use the last page of your sketch book or any spare sheet of paper to try out your pencils and discover the difference between HB and 6B. Look at the shading I have done opposite and do the same. Relax your wrist, practise starting with quite firm pressure and then gradually slacken off. You will find the secret is a supple wrist.

Try laying your ruler on the page and shading up to it.

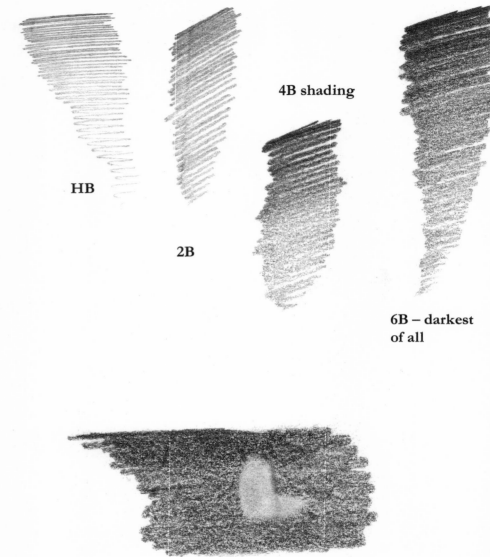

4B shading

HB

2B

6B – darkest of all

6B

4B

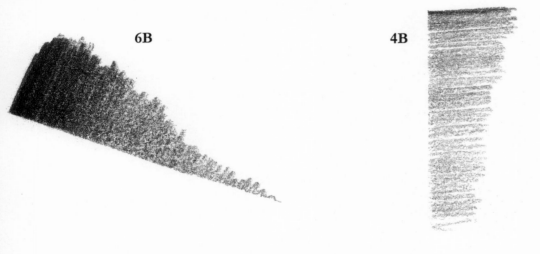

Finally use your rubber, but beware! Clean the rubber on a spare piece of paper after each use. In this way it won't make smudges on your work.

Have fun, and keep practising. The golden rule is a light touch and a supple wrist. See how dark you can make your shading, then release the pressure gradually to let it become lighter and lighter until it is hardly visible.

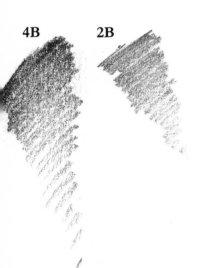

4B　　**2B**

The advantage of sketching in the home is that everything you want is at hand. Even if you have only thirty minutes to spare there is something you can do.

I don't want to impose anything on you, but remember that you are only just beginning. It is frustrating to choose a subject which is beyond you and make a mess of it. 'Oh I can't draw,' you'll say, but it isn't true. The problem is that you crossed over into the fast lane after the first driving lesson.

Why not try something simple, like a lamp shade or perhaps a part of a wooden chair? Not the whole chair, just a corner of the back of the chair. I have done the same lamp shade with different shading. Start by sketching in the lamp very lightly, so corrections are easy, and don't be afraid to use your rubber.

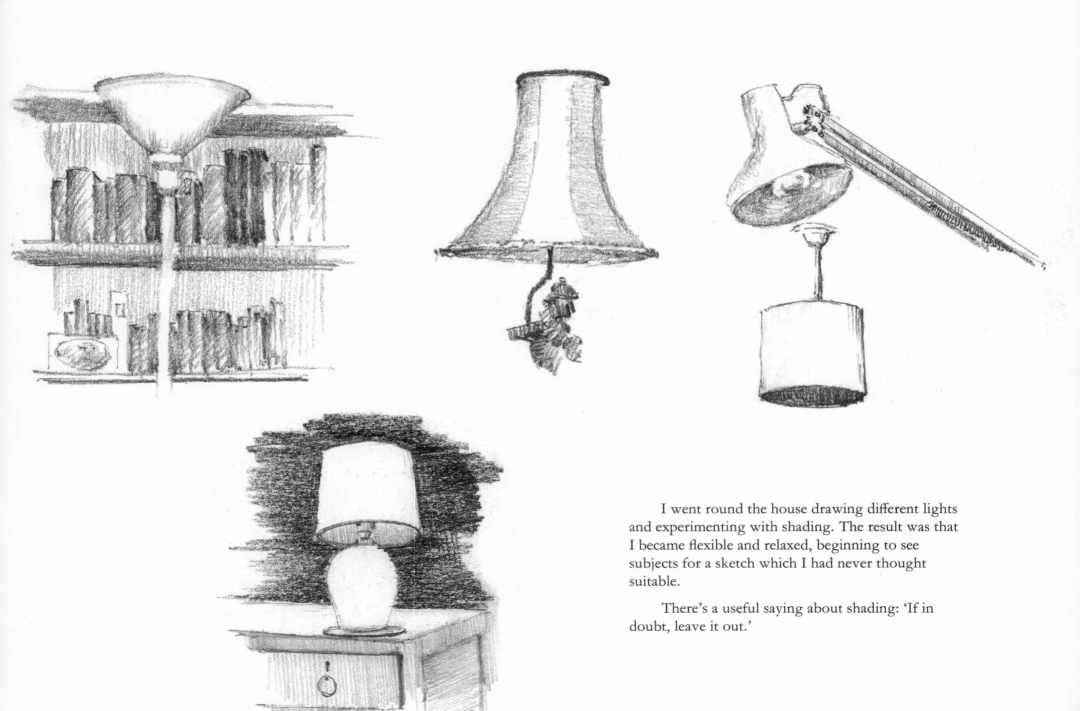

I went round the house drawing different lights and experimenting with shading. The result was that I became flexible and relaxed, beginning to see subjects for a sketch which I had never thought suitable.

There's a useful saying about shading: 'If in doubt, leave it out.'

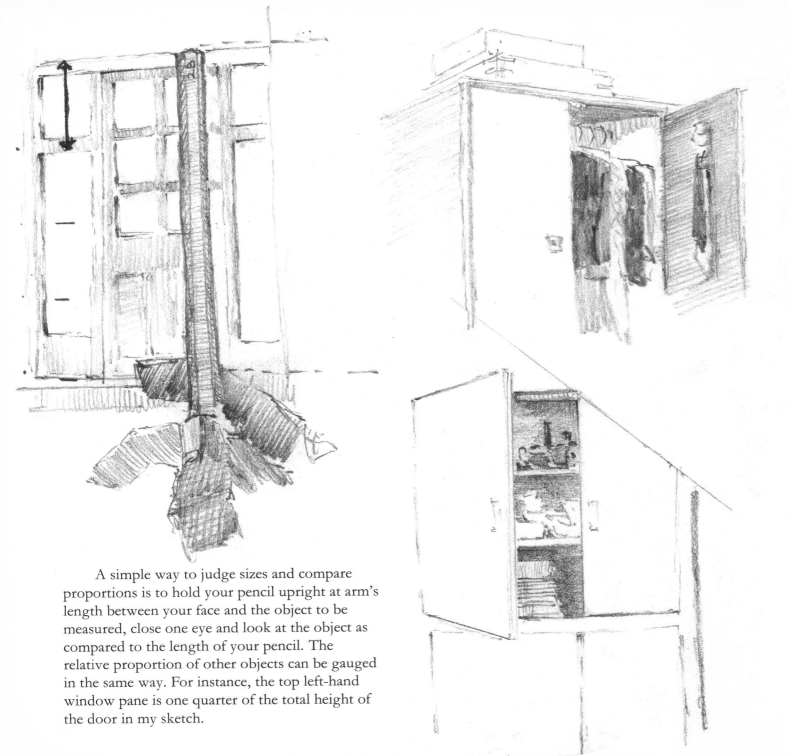

A simple way to judge sizes and compare proportions is to hold your pencil upright at arm's length between your face and the object to be measured, close one eye and look at the object as compared to the length of your pencil. The relative proportion of other objects can be gauged in the same way. For instance, the top left-hand window pane is one quarter of the total height of the door in my sketch.

Doors of all kinds are interesting and useful subjects for a drawing. (They are also good for practising perspective. Read on!)

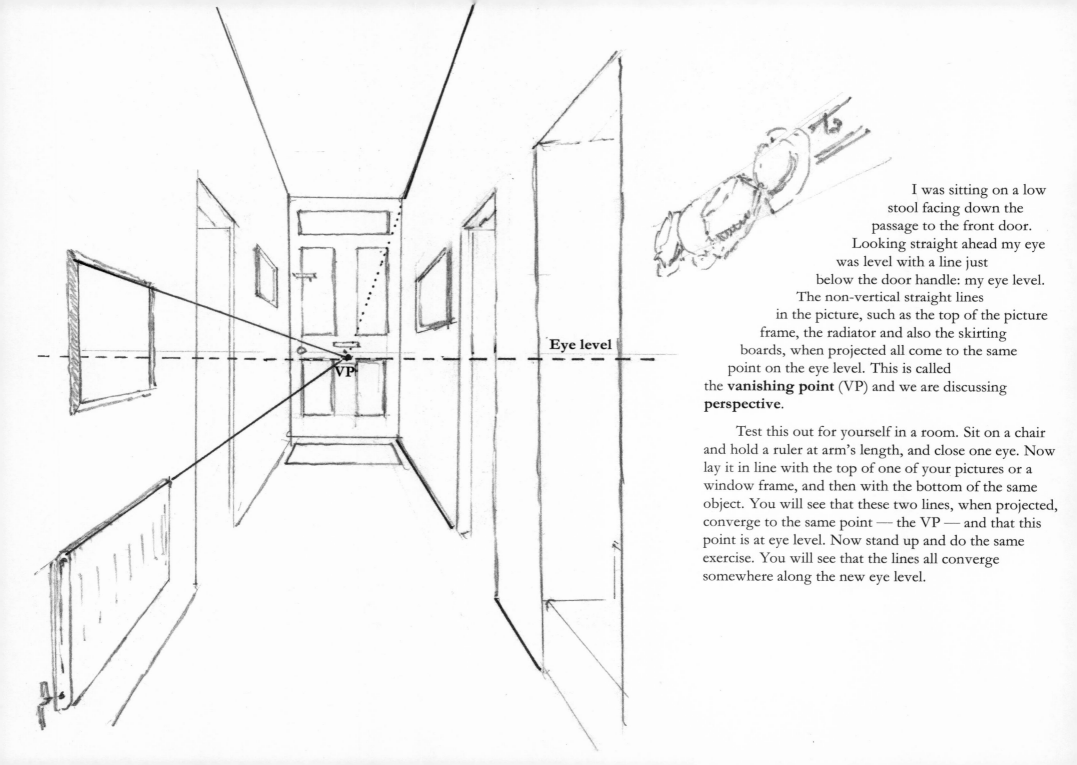

Eye level

VP

I was sitting on a low stool facing down the passage to the front door. Looking straight ahead my eye was level with a line just below the door handle: my eye level. The non-vertical straight lines in the picture, such as the top of the picture frame, the radiator and also the skirting boards, when projected all come to the same point on the eye level. This is called the **vanishing point** (VP) and we are discussing **perspective**.

Test this out for yourself in a room. Sit on a chair and hold a ruler at arm's length, and close one eye. Now lay it in line with the top of one of your pictures or a window frame, and then with the bottom of the same object. You will see that these two lines, when projected, converge to the same point — the VP — and that this point is at eye level. Now stand up and do the same exercise. You will see that the lines all converge somewhere along the new eye level.

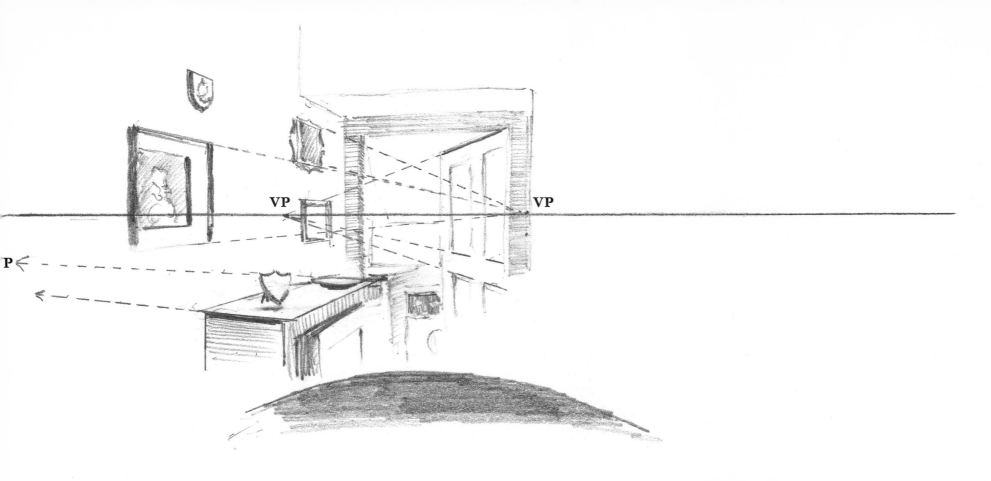

I sat at a table looking towards the door into the kitchen, and drew some of the objects around me. The dark horizontal line shows my eye level. The pictures on the wall to the left all lead my eye to a VP straight ahead. The partly open door led off to a VP to the left, but again somewhere on the eye level. The top of the cabinet led off to a VP a long way to the left, but again at eye level.

Try to do this yourself. Sit not exactly in the centre of a room, facing a wall. Look straight ahead and make a mental note of the line of your eye level. Very faintly draw in this line and make a sketch of the scene before you, being sure to include pictures and perhaps a window on the left or right. Now stop drawing and by laying your ruler along the top and bottom of any pictures or windows you have drawn, see if the lines converge to a VP. Don't be disheartened if they don't; in time perspective will become second nature.

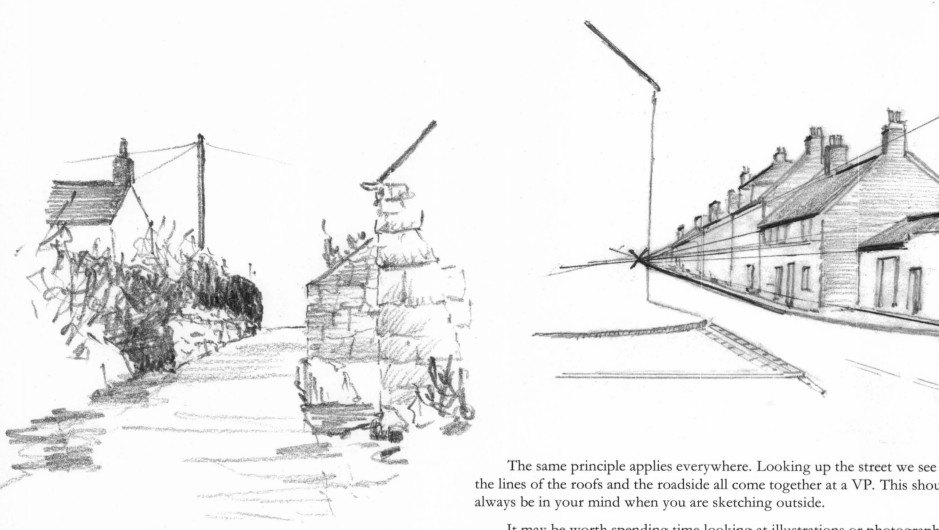

The same principle applies everywhere. Looking up the street we see that the lines of the roofs and the roadside all come together at a VP. This should always be in your mind when you are sketching outside.

It may be worth spending time looking at illustrations or photographs of buildings and laying a ruler along all the lines that are not vertical, and see where they meet. Try this sometime. It is probably the best way to fix perspective in your mind. Once you have mastered the principle, you will never be intimidated again by the word perspective.

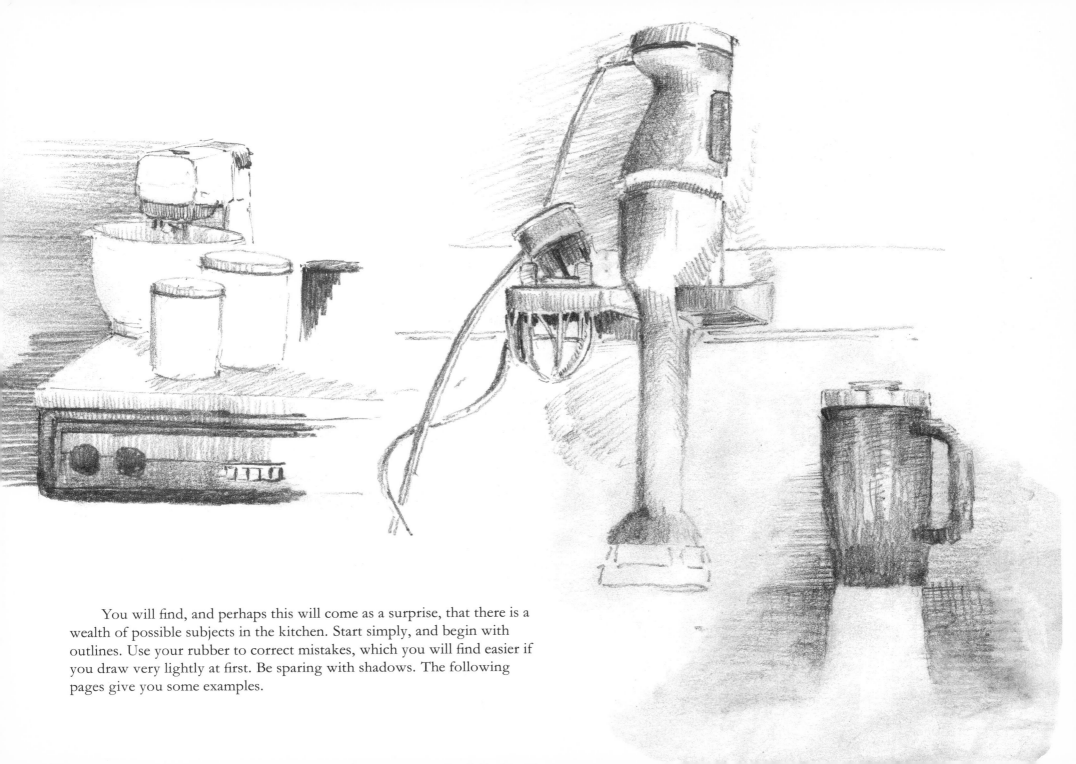

You will find, and perhaps this will come as a surprise, that there is a
wealth of possible subjects in the kitchen. Start simply, and begin with
outlines. Use your rubber to correct mistakes, which you will find easier if
you draw very lightly at first. Be sparing with shadows. The following
pages give you some examples.

From where you happen to be sitting you will find all kinds of objects that are interesting to draw. Just sketch away with a light touch using an HB or 2B pencil. Contrary to what many people think, I never have any hesitation in using my rubber, but avoid taking out heavy shading or you will smudge your work. — So, start off lightly and satisfy yourself that your outline is correct before doing any heavy shading. If you must remove some dark pencil work, for instance, when putting in highlights, clean your rubber after each stroke.

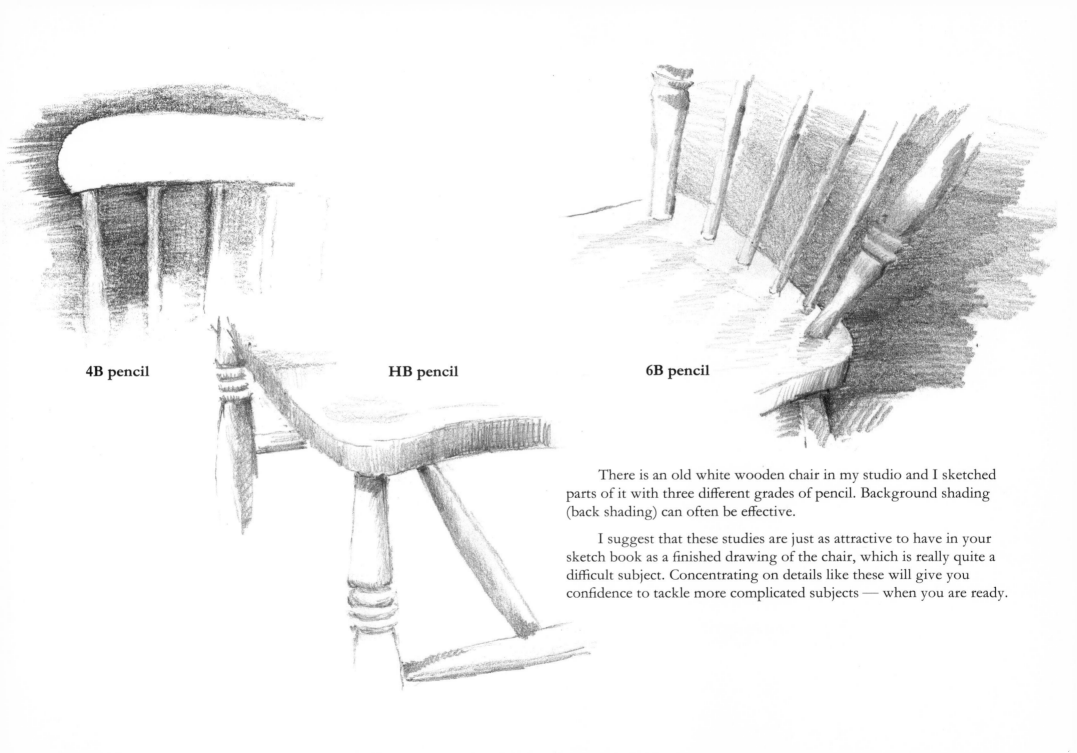

4B pencil

HB pencil

6B pencil

There is an old white wooden chair in my studio and I sketched parts of it with three different grades of pencil. Background shading (back shading) can often be effective.

I suggest that these studies are just as attractive to have in your sketch book as a finished drawing of the chair, which is really quite a difficult subject. Concentrating on details like these will give you confidence to tackle more complicated subjects — when you are ready.

Still-life still has to live! Whether it is a collection of bottles or a bowl of fruit, it is either alive or it is flat. So how do we go about tackling a bowl of assorted fruits?

I suggest that you spend a moment or two composing the fruit, and noticing how the light falls on the surfaces. Try not to complicate the subject, which is already quite challenging.

Personally, I spend quite a long time endeavouring to draw the outline accurately and to scale. This I do with a very light touch, using an HB or a 2B pencil, and my rubber.

Have you ever thought of looking at what you have done through a mirror? It is an excellent way to check on your ability in handling shapes and symmetry. Why not find a hand mirror now and look at what you have done. It is surprising how errors show up if you reverse the image.

Here is the second stage in my still-life drawing. I have begun to put in the deeper shadows, but have not concentrated on any one piece of fruit. I am endeavouring to keep a balance. The bowl is formed of elaborate and highly coloured tracery, but you will see that I don't want it to dominate.

This is the last stage. It is always a problem to know when to stop, and if there is any advice I can give, it would be to stop too early rather than too late. There is a temptation to fiddle with a pencil and this can often spoil your picture. Here, the bowl is almost as detailed as the fruit. Any more detail on the bowl would bring the eye down from the fruit to concentrate on the bowl — and the subject of the sketch would be lost.

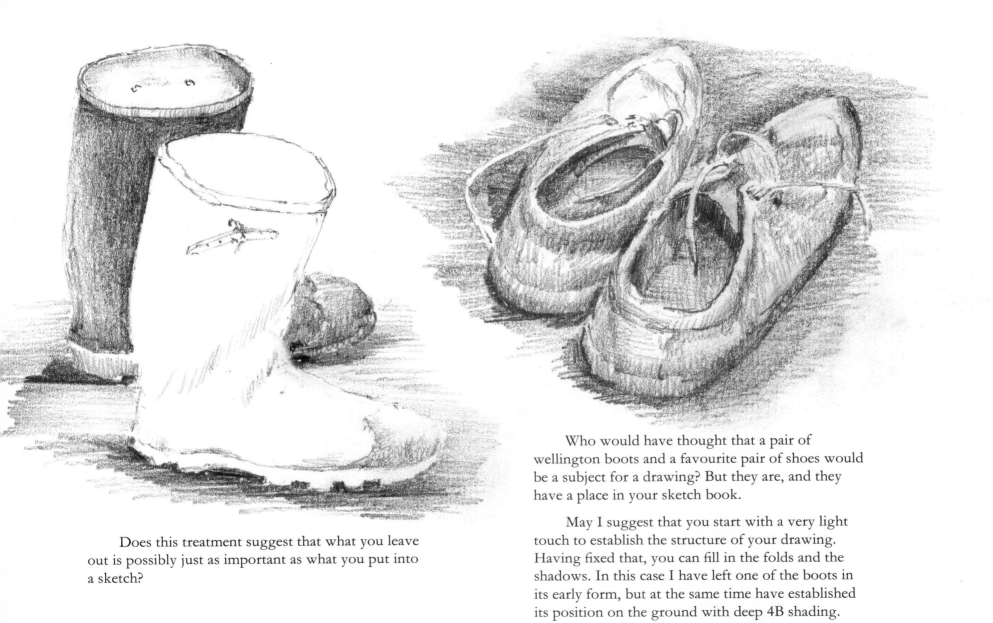

Does this treatment suggest that what you leave out is possibly just as important as what you put into a sketch?

Who would have thought that a pair of wellington boots and a favourite pair of shoes would be a subject for a drawing? But they are, and they have a place in your sketch book.

May I suggest that you start with a very light touch to establish the structure of your drawing. Having fixed that, you can fill in the folds and the shadows. In this case I have left one of the boots in its early form, but at the same time have established its position on the ground with deep 4B shading.

Most of us have a collection of torches at home and they can be an interesting subject, though they are not particularly easy to draw. To check the overall accuracy I looked at my drawing through a mirror.

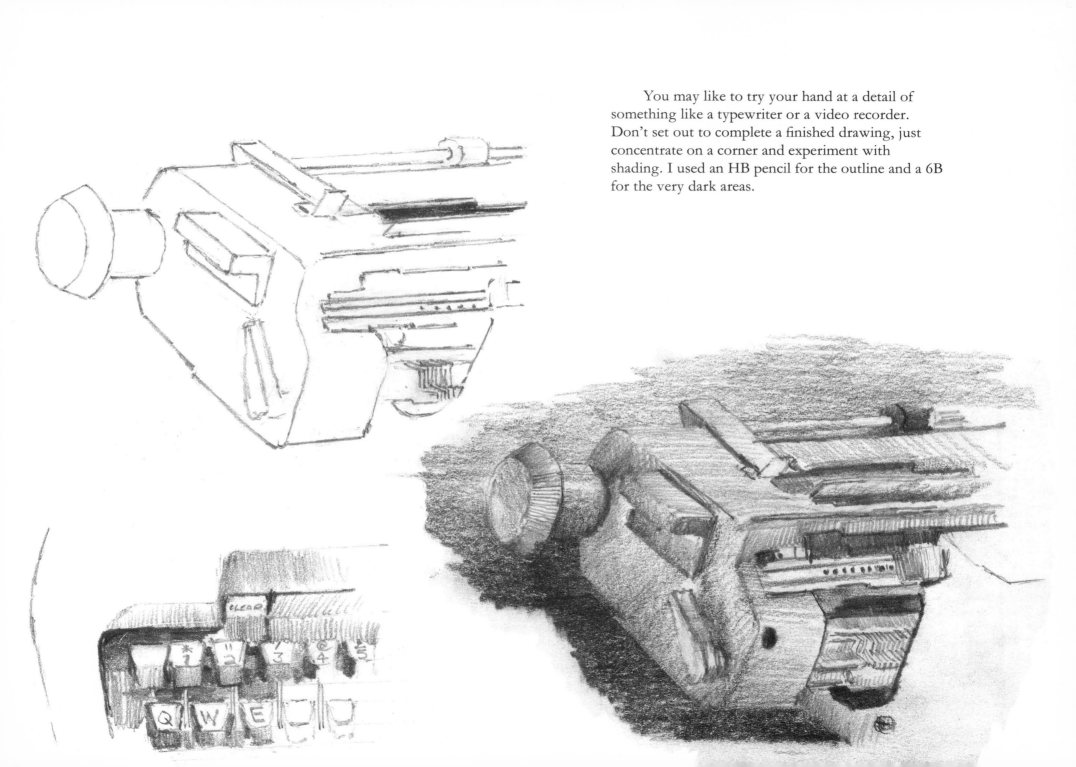

You may like to try your hand at a detail of
something like a typewriter or a video recorder.
Don't set out to complete a finished drawing, just
concentrate on a corner and experiment with
shading. I used an HB pencil for the outline and a 6B
for the very dark areas.

Notice how this sketch has been built up.

I started with very faint outlines which established the structure of the instrument and the telephone directory beneath it (but I had to make good use of my rubber before I got it right!). All this was with a 2B pencil. Shading began with the darkest shadows with a 4B, but I have left one side unshaded to show you how it developed. Think about the effectiveness of the heavy shading (and the direction of the lines of the pencil) against the outline of the book.

Finally, don't forget to practise your shading exercises. They will help you to achieve a supple wrist and lightness of touch.

If you want to try your hand at a table lamp illuminating a room, remember that the area surrounding the light must be darker than the light source. In the sketches on this and the following page I have chosen the light as the focal point of the drawing with the shadows giving strength to the surrounding area. Once again it is important to stress that a light touch at the start with an HB pencil will help you to design the layout.

Notice how the light stands out against the darker background.

I sketched an attractive oval window in a friend's house and then decided to incorporate it into a little drawing of that corner of the room. Notice the different treatment, for had I used the same strength of shading it would have intruded into the composition. As it is, the room is light and airy.

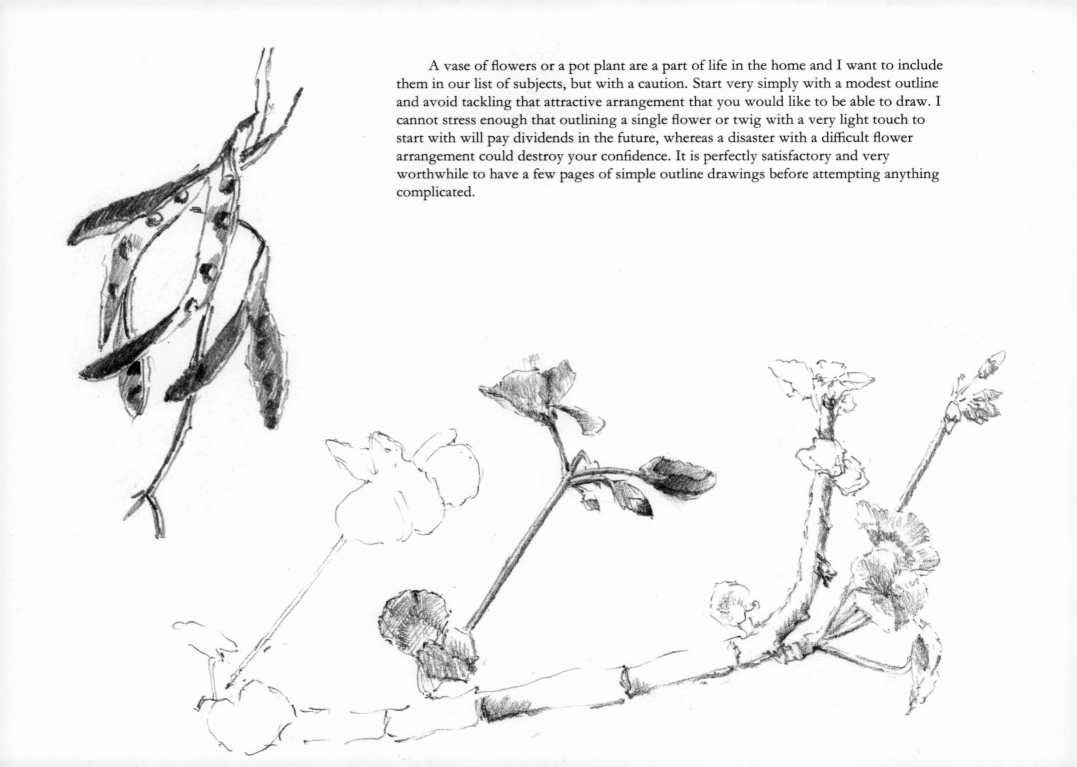

A vase of flowers or a pot plant are a part of life in the home and I want to include them in our list of subjects, but with a caution. Start very simply with a modest outline and avoid tackling that attractive arrangement that you would like to be able to draw. I cannot stress enough that outlining a single flower or twig with a very light touch to start with will pay dividends in the future, whereas a disaster with a difficult flower arrangement could destroy your confidence. It is perfectly satisfactory and very worthwhile to have a few pages of simple outline drawings before attempting anything complicated.

I sketched the outline of this cyclamen, trying to be accurate. It was a light pink flower against a darker background and I decided to use a 4B pencil to give some depth to this. Notice that I have graded my shading. I used a rubber to pick out the highlights — cleaning it after each stroke.

Sketches of single flowers
will make an attractive page in
your sketch book.

Foxglove.

Be sure to draw a very light
outline of each leaf and flower
before you attempt to go on to
heavier shading.

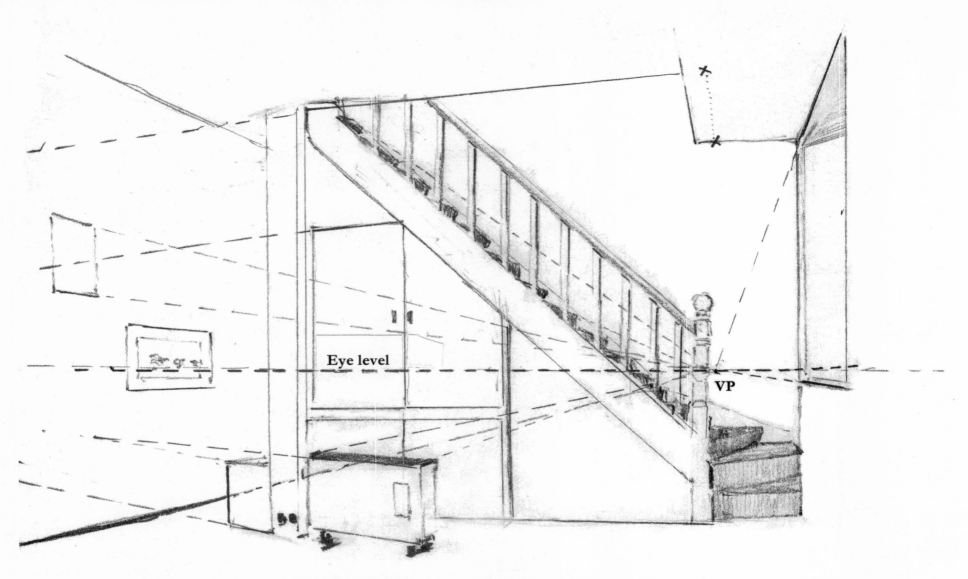

Eye level

VP

Stairs are intriguing subjects, whether drawn from above or below, and pose their own problems of perspective. In the earlier discussion of perspective, I said that there could be more than one vanishing point: here is an example. I was sitting on a chair and my eye level was as shown. However, if you look to the left you will see that the cupboard door, the electric heater and the ceiling above the stairs all project naturally towards the left to a VP along the eye level, but a long way beyond the drawing. The rest of the drawing leads you down to the central VP. Experiment with this, holding out a long ruler against non-vertical straight edges of items in the room. You will see how it all works out.

Here is the completed sketch. Lay a ruler along all the non-vertical lines and see whether you can find the vanishing points. Does my drawing reflect accurately what I have been saying?

Shading has played an important part. The first sketch which was completely flat established the position of the different angles in the room. When I began I used the small area between the Xs on the earlier sketch as my measuring scale. Holding my pencil upright at arm's length I measured that small piece of wall, then found that the handrail was five times as long, the top of the under-stair cupboard just slightly longer than my scale, and so on. The composition could have been improved by including a chair or a small table in the foreground but I have resisted doing this so as to make this a clear perspective exercise.

This little sketch shows how the line of
the shelving, when extended to the right, will come
to a point at eye level. Before you start to
draw in the details, spend a little time
ensuring that the outline is correct.
Shading will be much easier if you have sketched in the main features with a very light
touch. Once this is done you can bring it all to life with a 4B pencil.

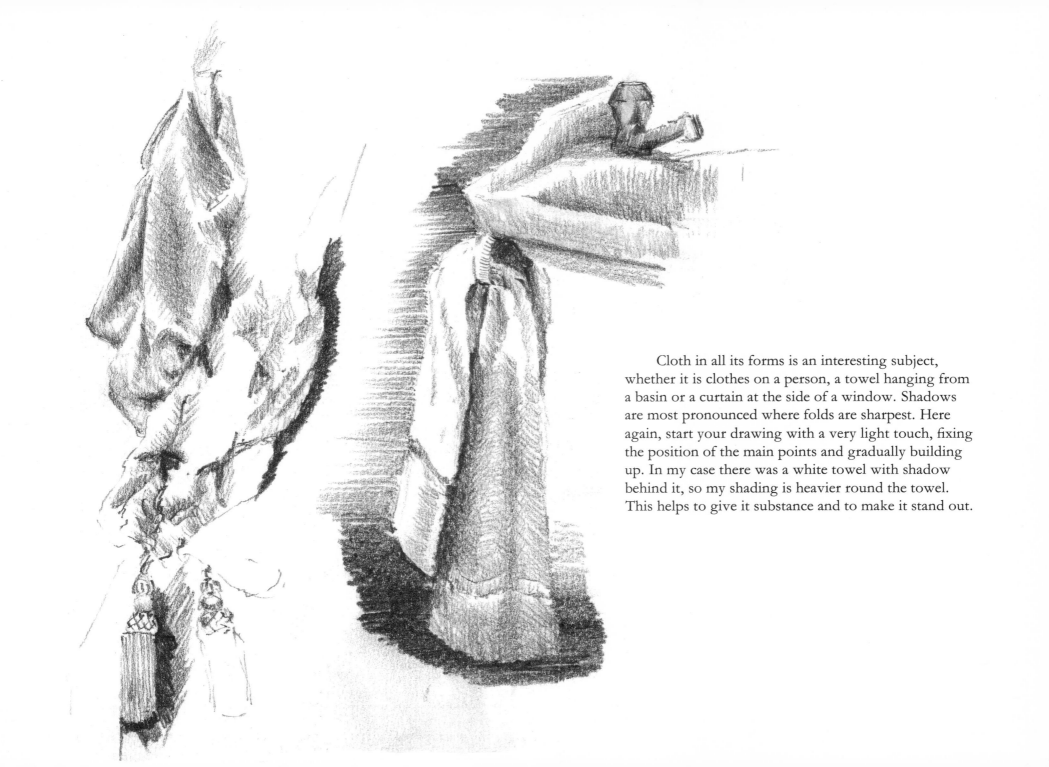

Cloth in all its forms is an interesting subject, whether it is clothes on a person, a towel hanging from a basin or a curtain at the side of a window. Shadows are most pronounced where folds are sharpest. Here again, start your drawing with a very light touch, fixing the position of the main points and gradually building up. In my case there was a white towel with shadow behind it, so my shading is heavier round the towel. This helps to give it substance and to make it stand out.

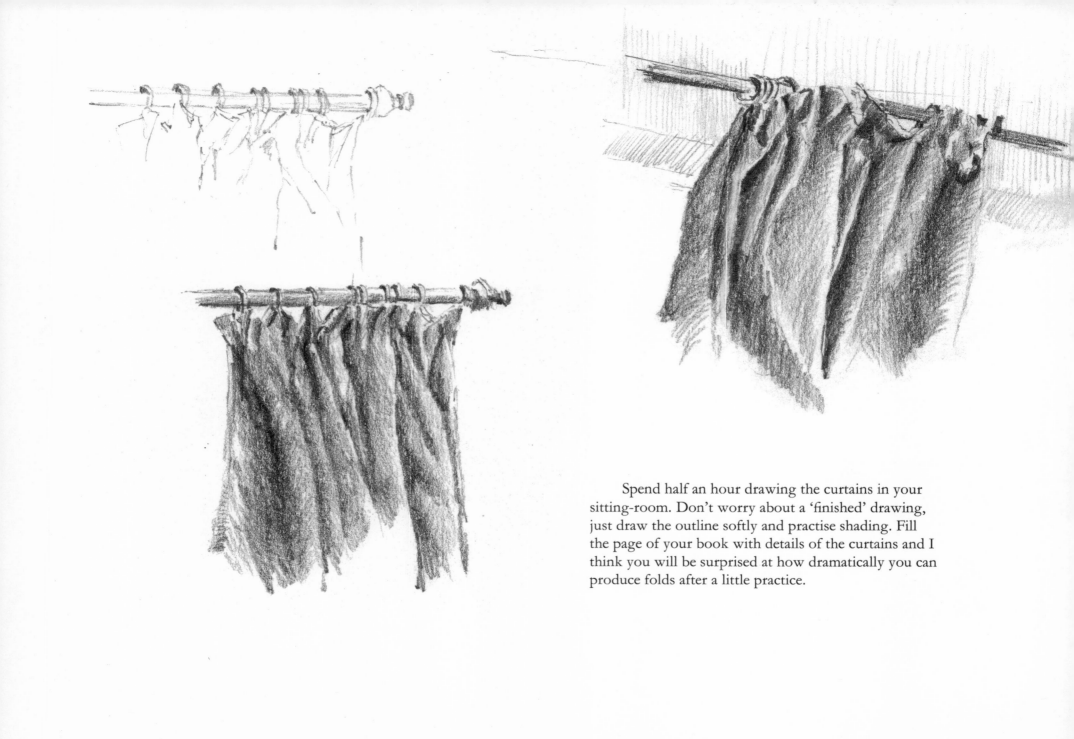

Spend half an hour drawing the curtains in your sitting-room. Don't worry about a 'finished' drawing, just draw the outline softly and practise shading. Fill the page of your book with details of the curtains and I think you will be surprised at how dramatically you can produce folds after a little practice.

Even the bathroom has possibilities and you will be tackling a number of problems here. Sketch in outline first and build up your shading later to make the individual objects stand out.

I think most families have 'special people', and I
am sure that they have a place in our sketch book.

A teapot and cup are a deceptively easy subject. You will need to make many alterations before the proportions are acceptable. This was patterned white china, so deep shading of the two objects was not possible. I used a 6B to obtain a strong background and bring the objects forward.

Spend a few moments practising outlines both of the cups and the handle. Remember to draw very lightly, really hardly visible, while you are trying to master these balanced curves.

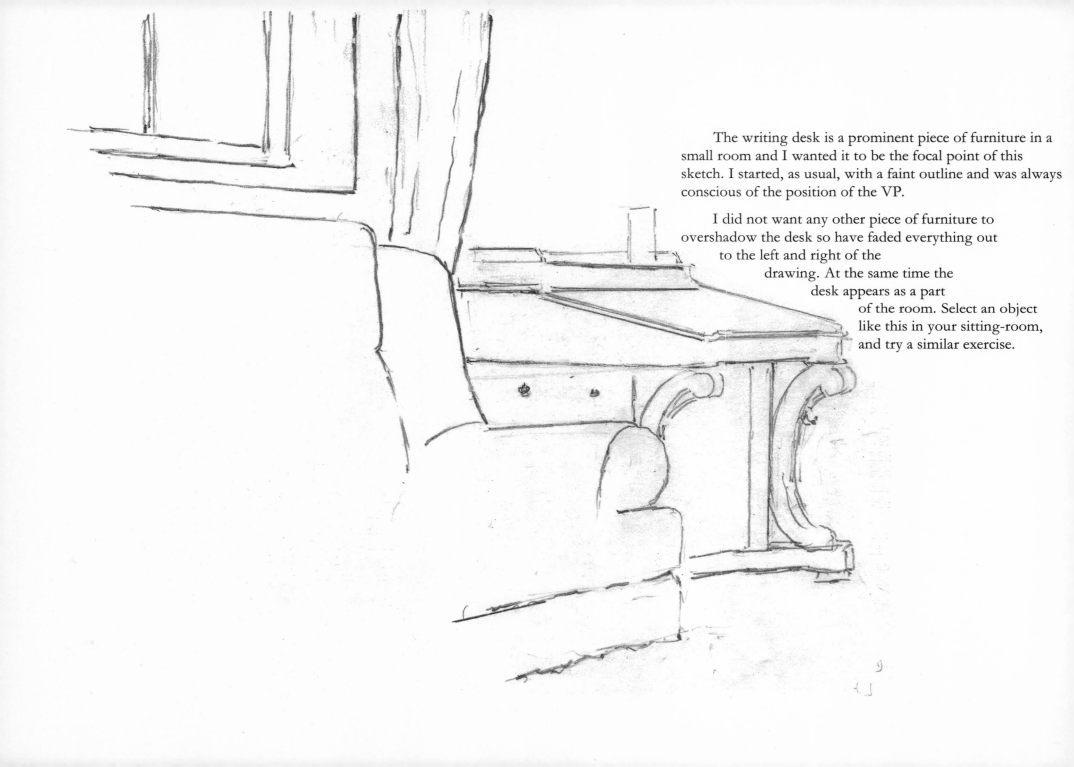

The writing desk is a prominent piece of furniture in a small room and I wanted it to be the focal point of this sketch. I started, as usual, with a faint outline and was always conscious of the position of the VP.

I did not want any other piece of furniture to overshadow the desk so have faded everything out to the left and right of the drawing. At the same time the desk appears as a part of the room. Select an object like this in your sitting-room, and try a similar exercise.

I liked the large onion in the garden trug, so I sketched it in, together with the outlines of the surrounding vegetables but concentrating on the central onion and working outwards. In no way is this a balanced drawing and I let it fade out when I had established the central theme.

It is a good exercise and means you can draw some object that attracts you, and after placing it in its surroundings, can leave the rest to the imagination.

This is a detail from a lovely garden at the side of a house. It would have been difficult to bring the whole scene to life so I settled for a detail: the fuchsia climbing up the wall from an old flower pot.

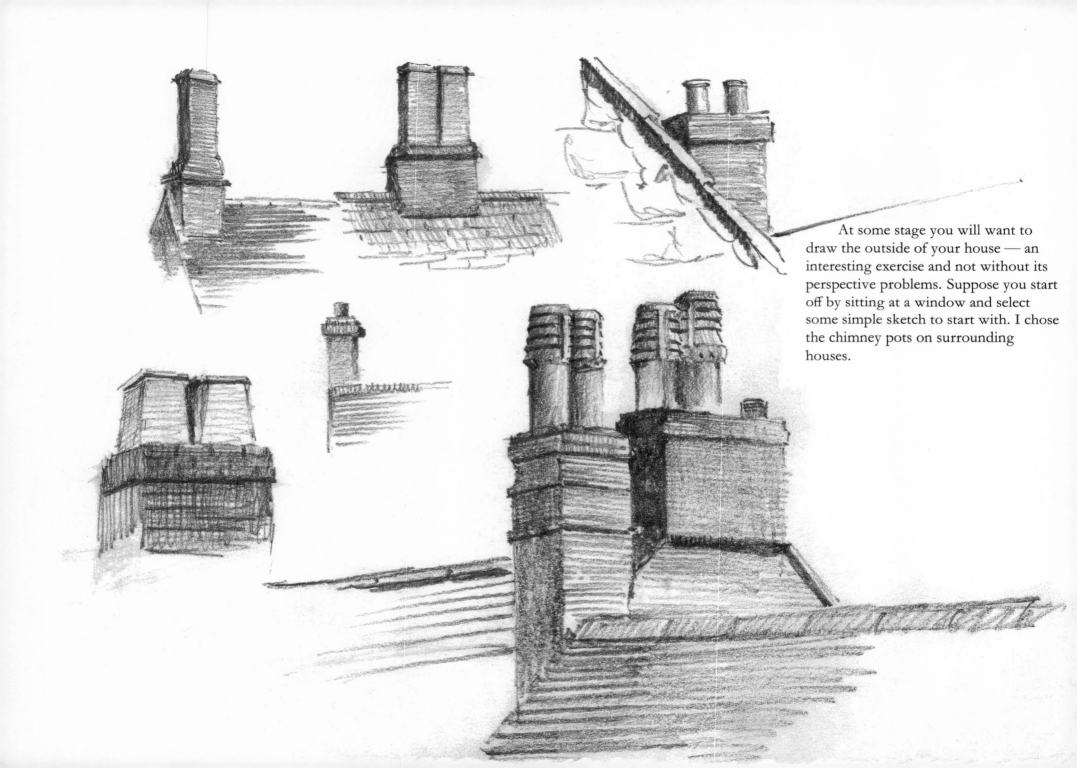

At some stage you will want to draw the outside of your house — an interesting exercise and not without its perspective problems. Suppose you start off by sitting at a window and select some simple sketch to start with. I chose the chimney pots on surrounding houses.

Once again I suggest that before you attempt a complete sketch of your home from the outside, you spend a little time on details of the building. Just fill a page with simple sketches. They will be a pleasing addition to your sketch book and will make you think about structure, but more important still, they will give you confidence.

Try a complete sketch of the outside of your house — but again, don't aim to produce a 'finished' drawing: the essential features are all that you should attempt at this stage.

At first sight this wooden structure at the back of a cottage might not seem a useful subject for a sketch, but I think it is. The shading inside the door gives a feeling of depth, and you will notice that I have decided to leave out the detail in the foreground to the right of the path, which was green grass.

Try to avoid the temptation to fiddle with extra shading; it is not necessary and will spoil your drawing.

Practise drawing your house from different angles,
leaving the adjoining buildings to fade out.

Whether you have a large garden, a small patio or just a window box, it will provide a subject for a sketch. This is a drawing of a very cleverly designed blaze of colour in a minute courtyard. If I had put in all the brickwork and every stem and leaf it would have become top heavy and would have missed the impression of brightness and colour that I wanted to give.

There is no single and correct approach to drawing — and certainly a pencil is not the only medium available. All of us are attracted to a particular style and if you feel happier with a stick of charcoal or a drawing pen, that's fine, use them.

I am convinced that more people give up drawing because they attempt a subject that is beyond them than for any other reason. That is why I have suggested you make a start with simple sketches of everyday objects around the house. Take it as a matter of course that with only a little time to spare you will soon be able to produce pleasing sketches. You will find it relaxing and enjoyable, just as I do, and a good way to build up your confidence.